Makeshift

B.A. McRae

© 2021 by B.A. McRae

All rights reserved.

ISBN | 9780578895116

"Stay groovy and good to yourself"
-B.A. McRae

Hand Whistles at Midnight

We were neglected messes of our own, searching for new pledges of a life beyond societal fences as we walked secretly through the equally neglected farm fields.

Our souls were louder than our voices as we discussed the world in our limited knowledge, and we let our imagination fill in the rest; I'm sure someday the brass truth will be revealed.

For now, I know this field is abandoned and that the night sky is beautiful, but it doesn't make the best light for walking.

It was left like us: dry of attention and crumbling without question; but what the farmers failed to mention is we're not going without a fight, we're not stalling.

The perspective we have on the world is ours to hold, and we have broken away from the mold of what we have been told to do with the appearing short time we have on this Earth.

My birth wasn't planned but man I'll be damned if I don't construct and plan the unconventional life, I'm worth.

If the world is so big, and life is so vast then why I ask is society so fast to broadcast its own casting list of the roles you must have, the characteristics you must possess in order to be deemed a success; where is the creativity in creating your own journey?

Every human is unique yet its options are bleak, but it's time we seek our own ways and techniques; sometimes I worry of setting out on this lively rebellion because society is hardly full of mercy but I remember it's up to me to make my life worthy, and if the world is going to be my jury then I'm giving them a hell of a story.

Like right now, as we're no longer whispering but howling our inspiring perspectives to the withered crops and the milky way, we heard a train whistle not too far away.

Our eyes were matching with wide spontaneous intensity as we started running towards the journey we swore to, today.

The train whistle's sound had whittled words rattling within its harsh melody as it grew more intensely the closer, we got; it echoed through the soles in our shoes to the souls in our chest.

The slowed down box carts rolling by, we waved goodbye to the field that witnessed our revelation and wished it fortunes of no longer being dry, this wasn't a solution to the revolution of our future but it'll be an interesting part of the story of how we got there; the night sky wasn't the best light but it made for quite the guest.

We'll ride in this old wood for a while, we'll narrate our dreams out loud, we'll make whistles with our hands.

We're on our way to greater things, this life will be the best thing I never planned.

Out Loud Clouds

The first time she gathered me in her arms it felt so natural it almost scared me.

I wasn't used to being held so delicately and with such sincerity in her certainty.

London's vague fog clouded my days in more ways than it usually did the year our lives intertwined.

My atmosphere's forced grey had nothing on the way her presence would shift the very essence of a room, to this ability she seemed to be blind; in the kindest way, she didn't have other's in mind, she was in the midst of being self-redefined and leaving the past behind.

I was a young writer, both literarily and financially poor, looking for an adventurous score so I could write some more.

I would try out different scenes of night life every night, trying to find where I felt right and inspiration to write, and the one night when I didn't care what I wore and probably made the general public's eyes sore I saw the face my eyes and soul would grow quickly to adore; she came through the music club door like she was walking into a bookstore, everyone else she could ignore she knew what she came here for.

She came to dance, which I later found out was her grand escape.

As a writer I find I romanticize things easily but pleasantly I couldn't deny her motor skills were a little dry, her articulation for rhythm wasn't very high, but it was the way she wasn't shy that made my heart take an entirely different shape.

She saw I was slightly watching as I was nursing a barely fleeting alcoholic bleeding drink and she motioned me to start dancing.

Laughing I shook my head and said I was writing instead, and apparently that was intriguing.

Once the music was over, we walked outside together and discovered though it was late in the night we both biked; our bikes were locked next to each other and I laughed with her as she playfully announced her hunger.

Technically we met in the nightlife scene, but I'd like to think we really met each other on that bike ride to the twenty-four-hour diner.

I learned about her love for dancing,

She discovered my need for writing.

She told me, ironically, that somedays she forgets to talk out loud.

As I disclosed, though my logic opposed, sometimes I tried way too hard to find some kind of shape or meaning in the clouds.

We biked a little ways to our destination, ready for some immobilized conversation and digestion; the dim-lit mediocracy was the perfect place to fall for someone so bright and extraordinary.

She was like a library of imagery with all her life stories, and I was more like a dictionary ever so slightly timely adding in my vocabulary which surprisingly made her smile; I always felt like an unnecessary addition to society but she made living feel revolutionary.

After hours of deep questions and random laughing sessions, we paid our bill and walked outside, where she daringly pulled me into her arms and I felt my pride step aside; for she made me feel safe in her small but large embrace, with my memories overall this is the one I'll recall.

She was my dancing diner girl, and I may just be able to write after all.

Unowned Beauty

These trees are layered in the stories I've shared and secrets I've spilled from years of climbing their branches with platonic companions, climbing as high as we could go.

No matter who I was climbing with I always seemed to be the one to climb higher, not that it was my determined desire, I just wanted to see the world a little brighter and the taller branches provided views better than photos.

Each time I reached the bark of the highest branch the world was set on a delicate pause.

My imagination gave an applause, my heart withdrew its flaws, and my passions felt like they were given a cause.

Unowned beauty painted in memories,

The sky has remained loyal through the centuries.

I hope these trees outlive me,

Not to a depressing degree, but that someone else can also confide in and see what I see.

That these trees are embedded with lessons and the purest intentions with your attention.

Life hits different up in the branches, and its shaded leaves produce bigger questions.

Sunlight Majesty

I will decorate myself in sunlight and majesty because I know I am worthy.

I don't need the mercy or selfish currency from a source so intoxicatingly unsure of themselves they steal the shine and warmth from someone who was sturdy.

I cried to my shattered heart, I mourned over the pieces that no longer had a part; then it was time to start a new journey to grace into my new free.

It was time to summon a hero, and that was going to be me.

I refuse to be damaged by mere specks in my story, that no longer even know me, that couldn't see how truly wonderful I am.

And I'll be damned if my happiness is tainted and condemned by some coward hiding behind a sham.

My past self wouldn't believe me now when I say I'm not afraid of you, but my how I have flourished and grown.

Once your true colors had shown,

I embraced the unknown,

I took back the throne,

now you want more warmth and light but you have been outgrown,

my future will no longer be postponed,

let your actions sink into your bones

as your echoes finally reach back to you that you're alone.

For a while there it was rough, but I grew to be tough.

The sunlight wraps around me, my smile covers me completely as the truest words reach my rebirthed heart, and the world around me throws a parade because it was waiting for me to realize this part; I can call the coward's bluff, because I am more than enough.

Cold Confusion

My shoes are starting to fall apart, I don't remember the last time that seemed to be a problem; I was probably a child.

I've been walking a lot more often though, even as it starts to snow, but it's a productive way to avoid compiling questions others want to know; and for that bit of time, the right and left side of my mind is somewhat reconciled.

Why do me and the dead of winter have more in common than the summer?

The summer brings promises of warm hope and adventure, which seems to be something I sadly lack to give her; whereas winter and I are an inevitable cold and in our presence of melancholy wrapped in irony there's some beauty, but mostly we're just seasonal and emotional clutter that could be skipped over with some slumber.

I'm not really necessary.

Which was momentarily scary, but as I accepted that I am no romantic vision for the artistic visionaries, or daydreams of the contemporaries, I understood I was temporary; my fears felt arbitrary as did the temperature apparently, as I set out for my daily walk with the company of January.

The cold air overwhelmed my face and freaked out my lungs.

I know there's disappointment hiding somewhere in my heart, but I can't find the right words to articulate off my tongue.

I'm aware that I'm important to a small population but that's not a big enough realization to switch my life's narration.

But perhaps it would be best for the foundation of these surrounding generations if I was in some sort of makeshift isolation.

I'll tuck away somewhere with my ratted shoes; no decisions to choose.

A place with no news, with a single view that I find ways to be mediocrely amused, accompanied by cold, silent, but somehow mimicking statues.

Faceless things that somehow capture exactly who I am.

A mess of cold confusion, that even the winter will condemn.

Dopamine

I swear her veins were engraved with music notes; she has this smile that reels me in.

She was the part of the world I actually enjoyed, she picked me up at the void my mind at the time couldn't avoid; she had loving arms that made me want to begin.

Her essence made it seem like she had little fragments of lost stars in her lungs, for every breath she took she was glowing.

On second thought, maybe not, a star of course but she wasn't lost, her existence was entirely on purpose; she was ever-growing and showing society it couldn't keep up with her easily, she was overflowing.

So why on Earth would a soul seemingly not of this Earth need me?

Well, she doesn't need me.

She appreciates me,

admires me,

can be herself around me,

she calls me funny

I call her lovely,

I suppose you need to see that I don't need her either, there is no plea.

But that's the best part, she *wants* to be in my heart, and I *want* to admire the galaxy that lives in her presence.

She picked me up at the void, and we became a new fluorescence.

You will go from woman to woman your entire life,

trying to find me again,

even the tiniest speck,

but you will always come empty.

Because there is no one else like me.

And fifty years later as you sit with regret,

as your mind begins to forget,

you will never forget who I am

because I will always be the best thing that ever happened to you.

You will forget some memories,

some days of your life,

but you will never forget the day you broke my heart and sent me away,

and the day you came back and begged me to stay:

what a foolish soul you are but I don't feel sorry for you,

for I am the best love your heart ever knew.

Dancing with Ghosts

I've been dancing with ghosts that don't know how to leave, and on the contrary, I don't know how to let them go.

I watch the trees turn into the shadows I thought I abandoned miles ago.

If I wish to stop in my tracks and lie down on this forest's grass that is as damaged as I,

Why,

I hope then it will take me in and turn me into something beautiful, that will be nourished by the sky.

Maybe all the details of me will dissolve and flourish throughout this patch I lay on, is there enough good in me in theory to do so?

Or was the grass below me trying to grow and perhaps this is just another memento that I am no rainbow in a meadow; ghosts only stay attached to things that don't believe in their own tomorrow.

Matching

She was the love of my life, but in my life, there wasn't always love in it.

It's like she had a permit to uplift spirits, because before she found me, I was ready to quit.

And I didn't know it but to my amazement, she was on her last thread when we met.

I don't know what she saw in me, or if I'll ever see it, but the light I see in her I will forever be in debt.

It made her laugh to see me surprised.

And to be fair even a stranger would observingly swear from my expression I fell in love every time we locked eyes.

She didn't care for huge fancy things, but she'll always be a sucker for expensive desserts.

I didn't care for big crowds, but she'll always be the owner of the second ticket I acquire for every concert we desire to attend; and we don't try to blend in, sporting our cool matching shirts.

My favorite moments with her all seemed to have a common denominator.

She was wearing her yellow dress and her bright smile; she looked like an illustrator's dream, a navigator to greater matters, but all that really matters is she felt confident as her own happiness generator.

I remember the first time I had the honor to hug her, I loved the feeling, and I patiently waited until it was normal to hold her longer.

She remembers my favorite author, we're each other's emergency contact at the Doctors, we have matching ring fingers, and I'll never forget her coffee order.

She told me she's come a long way and she finally feels okay, and she intends to stay that way.

I gave her a reminder after congratulating her, that although of course I was here to cheer her on, she paved her own way; she deserves a bouquet every day, but she wouldn't accept that anyway, she'd rather go to the cafe.

I wonder what moment she sees when she's most in love with me, what did I say?

As for me and what I see, I was playfully chasing that wide-eyed girl with a laugh that froze the world, wearing that yellow dress that twirled around her legs that teasingly ran away.

My brain is serving dinner tonight.

Would you care for a plate of mush?

What do you want from me;

you want me to wish you the best?

Like I was nothing in your life but a guest?

I'm not going to do that;

I don't wish you anything.

I haven't seen everything,

isn't that something,

but I do know one thing.

I know what the rest of your life is going to be like;

not every detail, but the general gist of it.

I'll admit for a bit when you split,

I thought I couldn't do anything but quit

but goodness how quickly the goddess within me

grabbed hold of me and showed me

how lucky I am to be out of your pitied pit.

Let me break this down for you to perceive.

You had the best,

the best you'll ever receive.

So, the remainder of your life will simply be a plateau.

Not much to show,

or room to grow,

No change in tempo,

or an interesting tomorrow.

Not horrible,

not amazing.

a plateau of nothing.

Because you had the best,

and you threw it away,

like nothing.

So how could you be trusted to hold something valuable and full of life,

go on and handle your strife,

living in an endless tone of a boring,

self-absorbing,

no context hoarding,

buzzing.

Outgoing Mail at the Oak Post Office

The World was a bit too much lately.

Not necessarily that things were bad or that I was particularly sad, but to put it plainly:

Sometimes to catch the tide of a wanted vibe you have to go exploring.

The sky was painted the purest blue, the tree's eager grew as they knew the memories, we were about to make for us two, through the woods in its peace we would find a piece of the scene we were craving.

I want to pick a flower and press it between the pages of a book that have made me who I am today.

Or find a patch of trees that look like a curious welcome, to a paused reality, though that unfortunately can't be, but to adulthood's dismay we pretended anyway.

Time took a break as we began to make within our minds a world where it wouldn't mind letting us have a few hours away from it's confusing structure.

Because within this imagination was a whimsical fictional location where we were our own train of thought's conductor.

Pollen was on a shortage today, so the bees were spreading the sun's rays wrapped with new moments.

The wood's Sky was a present to the painters and its sounds were a gift to the poets.

Let's spot secret doors in the trees and buy stamps at the Oak Post Office,

We'll find big leaves to be our envelopes and write about this moment to the future us.

We'll ship them off in the flowing river and wave goodbye while laughing at the silliness of it all.

To embrace this large amount of celebration, we can stall while reality is on call.

"Do you ever think we'll stop learning words?"

"I should hope not, what a boring life that would be." Our answers and questions in the air hanging out with the birds.

Perhaps we can try to carry this new perspective out of here and into our daily lives.

The future was ready to jive as our feet arrived at our next drive; and if we open up and allow it reality has more than we think it can give.

Irony's Cot

But isn't it frustrating

that simultaneously

while we are living

there are moments of our lives we can't remember?

Decisions we've made,

even if they were tiny,

moments we lived yet we can't recall them even slightly;

our brains have subconsciously surrendered.

It's just frustrating is all,

almost overwhelming.

Irony lays itself deep,

in the fact

that, we don't see the blend

when remembering fades into forgetting.

Burnt Coffee

Drank coffee today that gave me the after taste of campfire.

Let me know if you hear of any taste buds for hire.

But seriously, how can this be; my brain's gone haywire and it's my heart's desire to feel a burning love more captivating then an entire fire.

I have to protect it because it doesn't even know it, that we're still under reconstruction from the prior buyer whom we thought was the angel of the choir, but once they got what they required they found a new supplier then off went the emotional gunfire.

It'll take weeks to convince the heart it isn't weak, but it'll take longer for the brain to get a clue what they should do; all over the mind they're putting up "*Who Can We Trust*" flyers.

The heart's got scars it fails to remember but the brain knows better; all the makeshift-swift stitches they've acquired.

Self-made repairs that were inflicted from who we depicted to be our true and deepest desire.

Though the heart and brain don't always balance well together on the same wire, they know how to label a liar.

Perhaps the heart will retire from love, and the brain will take on the responsibility of the necessity to rewire a new rectifier.

Because monsters don't wear identifiers, and though it'll take time for all the good to once again pump through my mind and soul's amplifiers, I'll stick with my coffee I don't need your company; I don't associate with liars.

My Best Days

Don't faze the daze

Be amazed

And let those thoughts ablaze

They're worth more than just wandering about the buzz in cafes

They deserve praise

Your imagination is above clichés

Whether you need to find yourself on the highway,

airway,

or railway

find a way to your pathway

I swear you're meant to be more than okay

Life has had its delays

But I hope you know;

you have been a part of the majority of my best days.

Be careful making impressions on my heart,

For I may end up loving you eternally.

You might just become my favorite part:

be careful making impressions on my heart,

for you may break it so effortlessly.

The Disguised Foreseen

I fell from a hell disguised as my haven,

it felt like I was falling forever but a safety net I landed in.

I got comfortable,

I felt safe and untouchable.

My heart was closed for years,

with no intention of coming back into business.

But everyone around me became my witness as I let it open again,

may my heart find me some forgiveness.

Because we didn't know,

why how could we with promises and love in place?

That sometimes embraces

turn into suitcases,

as the safety net is cut again,

and you can see it all on your face.

Why does this keep happening to me?

Always the devotee,

another deep scar on my heart that you can see, another heartbreak I could never foresee.

New Definitions

Glances stolen, in the kindest fashion, encompassed by melodies that knew their souls out and in.

In-depth souls shedding their patrols, releasing their passions no more rations for compassion.

Drifting along for so long, although they're still floating,

now there's an attachment to something.

Accompanied by fresh air and refreshing songs.

No limitations to their imagination's locations, in each other's company their realities were on vacation, and the topic of discussion was anything.

The sky had new meaning; the trees grew new definitions.

Pure ambitious missions of expeditions were in commission.

Their lives deserved unconventional propositions; let the world observe their radical traditions.

Glances treasured,

In the simplest measure.

Souls growing in their own separate tones, music laced in their bones, a growth all on their own.

In-depth souls in the comfiest company they've grown to known.

You say it feels like a lifetime ago:
then treat it like one.

Collective Sunshine

I saw so much of you,

where on Earth did you go.

I thought I knew you,

who did you turn into,

I don't even care to know;

my that was ages ago.

I'm entirely new myself,

thank goodness.

Newfound confidence

and reclaimed worthiness.

The world will be a witness

to my happiness.

This is the progress of my success;

you I no longer need to impress,

for I have always been my own kindness.

I thought we were a part of something special.

But after you left,

I learned my truest fundamental

that all along I was

the existential sentimental,

I held the potential

and life just couldn't see me settle.

I wrote you beautiful poems,

you could have cared less.

The words I write that truly matter

will always belong to me and my success.

I was wrapped up in your hands so tight,

now I'll never forget with all my might

that I can always find refuge in mine.

I will no longer be undermined,

you must be mistaken,

I am my own collective sunshine.

You threw us away like I didn't exist,
so, I did the same:
I moved on and I grew.
And as time flew
you finally realized what you threw,
and when you saw I took after you
and forgot about you,
well you didn't like that did you?

Wonderful Eyes

In your eyes

I see no disguise

of lies,

I still can't help but be surprised;

for I am not use to such a wonderful thing.

You genuinely want to see me smile;

with you I find myself smiling at everything.

I'm not making up excuses,

I've got a few different diseases here

trying to party at the same time:

sorry for the chaos.

I've had men promise me the world,

and oh how they take it back so easily.

Gave them all the colors I own,

and they took it away to paint a different scenery.

I'll never need a promise again,

because what I offer myself is more than you ever could,

and I'd never lie to get what I want.

My pretty face

and beautiful trace

will forever haunt that pitiful heart you try desperately to flaunt.

Alone at last,

alone thank goodness.

How could a goddess

bare to witness

such inner sadness?

How powerful love is, how easily shifting it can be.

For it blinded me to see,

how truly selfish you were for such simple compassions that are meant to be free.

Celebrated Souls

We met in December,

And now I know what my heart always knew but my mind didn't remember.

That our souls were made together.

In the beginning of our stories they were separated,

But now celebrated;

We were always meant to find each other.

Goodness me,

you should be the one who's sorry.

For I know the kind of royalty I was crowned to be.

And my destiny knew you weren't worthy

or true to me,

and bless it be

because my life will not be half-loved and run by someone;

this is my monarchy.

So, you should be sorry,

because my face and presence will forever be

living in the highlight reel of your life;

so, every time your mind glances through them you can be sorry

to the precious memory you'll never forget.

You'll forever be in debt with regret,

while I'm off living my best life yet.

Tuesday Night

"How are you doing my Dear?"

'Oh you know, just enjoying the atmosphere of being here.'

"Is it weird to say I miss you like crazy today?"

'Of course not, in fact, I feel the same way.'

"I'm glad we are both contently captivated by this overwhelmingly awesome love that doesn't have the justice of words."

'Oh my gosh you're such a nerd.'

"Yea yea, love you too."

'Oh stop you know I love you.'

"I know, your sarcasm can't be ignored, so what should we do I'm bored."

'Whatever you'd like, we can watch a movie, play some cards, put on your favorite record.'

"*My* favorite record, oh no, let's put on *your* favorite record; you're the one who has the good taste."

'Well I can't argue with you there, thank goodness I arrived when I did and came prepared and saved you from that toxic waste.'

"Easy now I still like some of that stuff, but enough of that, I'd like to ask you something if that's okay?"

'Of course, silly, what is it you'd like to say?'

"Actually, I'm sorry, I have to do something first real quick Darling."

'No need to be sorry Honey, I'll be excitedly waiting.'

"Your kind patients will be worth it."

'Very well, can I still sit?'

"Well for the moment while I put this record on yes, but then I'm going to have to politely ask you to stand."

'By all means, of course, please lend me a hand.'

"Alrighty, just let me lightly set the needle down and turn up the stereo."

'Wow, the last time I heard this song was so long ago.'

"May I please have this dance?"

'There's a slight chance.'

"There's that sassy sarcasm again."

'Just keeping you on your toes, you know I like to use it every now and then.'

"We are indeed quite silly."

'Slow dancing for no particular reason on a Tuesday night, why yes, I'd say we must be.'

"You know earlier when I said I was bored; I didn't mean I was bored of you or being around you."

'I know, I don't grow old of the view of you and your interesting tattoos either, ever since we met it seems life has always stored some kind of unexpected adventure; like the spontaneous dancing one we just slipped into.'

"You're adorable, here let me spin you."

'Oh I don't know about that, but wow you're quite smooth; look at us two!'

"We are quite the pair."

'I dare say we are; quirky and rare.'

"How many peculiar adventures do you think we'll have together?"

'I'd say however many adventures that can be packed into forever.'

Serotonin

Sometimes we would just drive around in the car, not necessarily far, which was perfectly fine for wandering minds like ours.

Simple, yes, and that seems to be our gist; it made me so happy that we could discuss theories of the Seven Wonders and our childhood Summers within the same 10 minutes, easily we could talk peacefully of eternity for hours.

One of the best parts was that talking wasn't always required.

It's as if when we were created, we were inspired and wired to admire and inquire the same things; all conversations expire, of course, to make way for new ones, but delighting in each other's company had no sign of being retired.

We were driving around for a while, exchanging music genres, stories, and smiles.

So many different album titles, a few different styles; this car has seen some classic, deep, alternative miles.

But now we've stopped the car; sometimes the engine gets a little too hot.

We were temporary residents of the empty parking lot.

Although, with it being empty,

why with the limits of our imagination it can be anything we want it to be!

After some tossed around ideas, we landed on an extravagant ballroom.

We pretended I was wearing pretentious perfume,

and they were in full 18th century costume.

We didn't '*stay*' in character the whole time per say;

It was just fun to start out that way.

The hot asphalt was our imaginative dance floor.

My phone speaker would do, as our music began to pour and roar in the accompaniment of our town's eyesore; the outdated and closed convenient store.

Conveniently for us, our shuffled music knew the vibe we were digging.

There wasn't a care that left our awkward moves that the cars flying by saw us dancing.

It didn't really cross my mind that this wasn't exactly what we had planned for today.

But meeting and connecting and loving each other wasn't on our life's agenda either, but I'd say we're pretty happy it turned out that way.

Things aren't perfect, and they shouldn't be.

What kind of high-pressure, fake life would that be; when would you know when you're truly happy?

Because yesterday was kind of a bummer, but today has a whole new hue of color; we're creating memories and being bold.

I'll take the days as they come, each and every one, because man

that smile will never get old.

Dusty Coat Check

She had runs in her nylons.

She never let me help her put her necklace on.

The only time she'd let me help her is when she needed a dancing partner to twirl her about her favorite song.

And even then, she was in her own world, and I was just fortunate enough to tag along.

She didn't think she was good at much, but I swear everything she touched was amazing.

She may not think she can do anything but to me she is everything, and I don't want her to pretend to be something I want the real thing.

I want to see her dancing with her eyes closed, not caring about her pose, even though God knows she could practically be photographed at any moment and it would be the spotlight of the gallery.

Maybe I'm the only photographer, I'll always be her admirer; this gallery is perfect, I'll never pick up my jacket from the coat check, that stubborn girl will always be special to me.

True Fiction

Sometimes I feel like an uninvited guest, to life.

Which I guess is alright, or I'm just being passive again and not putting up a fight; I don't feel like I've had enough time to get ready anyway, I could only find this light armor to deflect my strife.

Yea, now that I'm saying it out loud it sounds pretty bad.

I've been trying to act naturally, which is seriously funny, as if I'm not some pitiful original copy; I'm not the first nor last of being touched by the sweet sorrow of sometimes feeling sad.

Am I running in place?

I don't even think at the end of life's events I'd make the place for 2nd best, but not necessarily last; and at the awards ceremony you wouldn't be able to trace disappointment on my face.

Long ago I ditched false hope.

But I forgot to replace it and now as I sit, I can feel my desire growing smaller and it's getting harder to cope.

Sometimes I think people look at me like some impossible solution.

Alas I can be pretty melodramatic, that may just be my socially panicked unbiased opinion.

I just don't want to abruptly find out one day that I'm actually an extinct life desperately trying to live amongst the deserving.

In the lost and found box of my existence there'd lie my favorite long-sleeved shirt from my childhood, a pair of gloves that fit awfully good, and on more than one occasion my passion and self-esteem were found missing.

But these are just things to say, I'm sorry for crash landing on your day, I'll be okay to simply just exist.

There are still things to enjoy, I'm just acting like an ungrateful kid who got rid of their imagination, staring at a toy; I'm a cheerful pessimist.

To whom it may concern,

    I'm not really writing to anyone in particular, I guess I'm just writing to not feel lonely. Which in itself is kind of sad but it's better than going mad: my company consists of the waves crashing against this place, the circling light that continuously momentarily hits my face, a goldfish I've somehow kept alive, and me. I thought being a lighthouse keeper would be a little cooler. For the most part it is, it's just been difficult lately, hence this letter. Who thought I of all people would miss talking to people? Though I am grateful of the company of the occasional curious seagull. But they have hard opinions on things, they're not as openminded as you'd think. That's probably never crossed your mind, as you can see, my sanity has already started to sink. My goldfish on the other hand, why we're a riot when we get to talking. Though it never shuts up about the economy I look past that because it totally gets me: we always end up laughing. I've never named it. I don't know if its male or female and although I'd say we're close, to ask it that doesn't seem appropriate and now we're far past it. Anyway, I don't think I'd even find the right name to fit. So, it'll remain nameless, and I'll temporarily shamelessly declare it my best friend. Goodness gracious when is this job going to end. Well I best be off to tend to some chores. I'll most likely be writing you some more. Another empty worded letter to add to the ever-growing pile. Write you in a while my silent receiver, I hope one day these odd letters can make someone smile.

Sincerely,

The extremely bored lighthouse keeper

Misplaced Paint

The sounds of the night made me think of you.

Shutting car doors, softened laughs, creaky floors, shuttered photographs, the muffled voices of the drive thru.

Our adventures were many,

and yet there's still to be plenty.

We didn't need expensive tickets or priceless exhibits to transform our shared minutes into the best memories.

We were just cruising with the oncoming perfectly timed melodies, basking in our similarities, slowly but surely becoming each other's amenities.

Coming up with the silliest but best things to do.

There always seemed to be something slightly or entirely new to do with you.

I very much enjoy the thought of painting on your hands, with little colorful specks of paint on your face.

And when I'm done you can paint mine; we'll let them dry and then hold hands for the most imaginative embrace.

We are lovely people, now together it just feels darling.

You've given me kindness I didn't expect, heck, I didn't even know it existed; so, this is the feeling of coexistent loving and living.

I think we've both had grand desires for ourselves that were long overdue.

You needed to be held and told you were well then more than enough, and as for me it's the cliché stuff; I always wanted to be somebody's '*it was always you*'.

Forever, Now

We belong in a story that will be kind to us.

But we landed in the hands of an author who didn't see us that way.

They put us on a different bus,

we didn't meet that day.

The words written for us didn't match our feelings toward one another.

But we found a way to defy the writer-

Look now, we're not rhyming!

We've thrown the Author off; quick let's find each other!

Take cover!

No, no that was a distraction there's nothing coming our way.

What do you mean you have nothing to say?

No! No, we're rhyming again, the writer is back!

Why does my heart feel under attack...

Why can't I be with them, why don't you want me to be happy, I don't even know you!

Why do you get to tell me what to do....

Even if it takes a thousand lifetimes, I will find my way to them no matter what.

You can throw me in the ocean, make me lose my mind, make me battle through every war and disease of mankind, but this is one door you cannot shut.

Go ahead and make me rhyme, make me close myself off from the world, but the part of my brain that remembers them and the piece of my heart reserved for them, you will never touch.

I love them too much.

My story will not end the way you want it, I will find them and make them happy.

For that's what we deserve, a happy story.

Don't you get tired of changing these patterns and making us rhyme,

Why wouldn't you want to be the narrator for two characters so grateful to have each other?

Wondering when I'll see them again, even if for a short time.

You've tried to place others in my life, but to me there is not another.

My memories of them can't be taken away, no matter how much you try to write into my life and slip into my mind.

Now I notice your rhyming is off, are you having second thoughts, perhaps dare I say you're thinking of being kind?

I won't get my hopes up, I know how that usually goes.

I remind myself everyday what they look like, I wish I had something to admire like little mementos or photos.

But something feels off, I don't feel the same in this moment it almost feels like a weight has been taken off me.

Like chains released from me that I cannot see- and I don't have to stop my thoughts there, they can wander, I can freely do whatever-

This is the happiest moment, the happiest I could ever be in a single moment of time!

This story is for us, I'm dropping everything and running to them; forever with each other starts now.

The Christmas Party

I know you can tell I'm not doing that great and I hate that I can't properly articulate how I'm feeling; and now I'm rambling and worrying that if I try to explain, the point will be missed or dismissed.

I can't put my mind to rest, the best analogy I can think of, is this:

There's a Christmas party, lots of activities, festivities, cookies, music to enjoy, and people to mingle with, and though there are lots of possibilities you admit you're a little bored.

You ignore the eggnog you've just been poured and go on to explore the gingerbread man decorating table you began to walk toward.

Sitting down and admiring all the little candies and frosting to use for decorating, you start pondering which gingerbread man to choose and pursue.

Sifting through the fragile pile you picked the best one for you.

When you sat down you had the purest of intentions.

Marveling at all the possibilities, every detail was given the utmost special attention, to see the progress and result there was pure joy and anticipation.

But it becomes more tedious than fun after a while, perhaps you were too ambitious.

The sweet choices that lay before you no longer seem so delicious.

All the while the sounds of the Christmas party are floating about, making you envision the fun you could be having instead of focusing on this annoying gingerbread man.

You think of the other gingerbread men in the pile you could have chosen, maybe you picked the wrong one, or the eggnog you passed up on, that could have been fun, so eventually, you just say you're done; you leave the station you're at, you left what you began with not really another plan.

In mid decoration and fleeted inspiration, you go back to the party.

It only takes minutes for you to forget about the gingerbread man completely.

I'm sorry that's a messy analogy,

I'll try to clear it up to the best of my ability.

You're the guest at the Christmas party, and the party is the life you had or the life you actually want before our relationship began.

And I am the picked out gingerbread man.

I'm terrified that subconsciously you'll resent me for leaving behind things in your life, which I never told you to do but perhaps you thought I wanted you to.

And one day in your own messed up view you'll see what you grew into and abruptly leave, and I'll have no clue.

I'm afraid I'll be picked up with the best of intentions, I'll be viewed, adored, decorated, and held.

And in that hold, I'll become a taken for granted novelty that is left in mid-thought, in mid planning, without any indication or warning; all clarity withheld, not a word of sense spelled.

I'll be left cracked, used, underappreciated, midway decorated, feeling separated, devastated, and humiliated.

Scraping the fake loving decorating details off me as my reality reminds me that this isn't that complicated to gather, this should have been rather easily predicted; given my past, perhaps no obscure analogy is needed, I will always just be designated to be isolated.

Every Piece of Magic

The way I held her, the way she looked at me,

I don't care what anybody says they don't have to agree,

I know the love that radiates between our chipped hearts is unique all in its own; it's something this world has never seen.

Her smile laces and traces every molecule of dopamine that's entered onto my life's scene since the day she gracefully interrupted my reality's routine; when I shouted in dismay to the emotional storm clouds in my mind that wouldn't go away that I needed a better day she was exactly what I meant, beautifully wrapped serene.

She's every piece of magic I'll ever need.

I'll be her calm or her party, she can take the lead.

Truly I just want to make her happy, I want to see her succeed.

Life may make her weary, but my loyalty will always be more than guaranteed.

Let the world try to take her contagious laugh away and replace it with sad days.

I'll be right there to take her hand and twirl her into the company of the sun's rays and treat her to a tasty treat at the cafe, perhaps we'd even catch a play; the world will have its unpredictable days, but she may rest in knowing I will be her pleasant always.

When she holds me, I feel like I could go on to accomplish anything, and the look in her eyes seals it right there.

She's rare and she's well aware;

in my seconds I'll admire her,

I'll take the minutes to help her through,

the hours we'll create memories,

and I'll spend a lifetime showing her how much I care.

You make me want to shout a request to the world

for it to reevaluate its Seven Wonders

because clearly with you

there's something it largely missed.

For in the midst of these constant spinning days

you've twisted the definition of amaze:

though you don't require or desire it,

my dear,

you were created to be admired.

You're the most whimsical being that's ever

existed.

So Much More

I found that long ago I didn't know that I needed to grow;

I thought you were a one man show and I was your only source of audio.

You trapped me in your world in which I wasn't free,

Here's a memo for me:

> You may be afraid to go, but it's okay to find a new hello.

The possibilities ahead of me may paint themselves to be overwhelming.

But the sun remains consistent and patient with me as I then see it's actually rather exciting.

I can greet the new me happily with spontaneity and the empathy that was drained so carelessly from me; these eyes were meant to gaze upon beauty, this heart was meant to be warm and giddy.

From now on my attention will be picky, I will be my own committee of deciding who will keep me busy.

And as of right now that's me; I'm the one I've always been looking for.

Let the realization pore over my sore heart that I am not broken apart, I've just deserved so much more.

I'll happily hold you,
but for yourself you must remember.
I'm not the answer to your happiness,
it's something you must possess,
but we can support each other.

Haunted

We've known each other for so long, it's strange to try to recall our first encounter not that I even remember.

I shouldn't say we've known each other, you seem to know me, but I don't really know you in any matter.

You know the parts of me that are new, versions I grew into, you feel like such a part of me I assume what you say, and think are true.

But just because someone knows you well doesn't mean they're good for you.

You aren't always around, but when you are you really sink in deep.

You entangle in my own thoughts and reality, these awful fortunes of promise you intend to keep.

It's as if you claim you know the future, without any liable credentials.

But being told your messages over and over again for what seems like ages, sometimes it's hard to remember what my future actually resembles, I have to find my potential.

If we are one in the same, why are you playing this game?

For my mind hurts with your piercing yelling, awful creations of irrational explanations; we are such different imitations how can we share a name?

Sometimes you remind me that we aren't that much different, one is just awfully down and the other has more control then I presumed.

I'm the sad one, and this sadness inside that's copied me and no longer takes its time to hide is seeking me out to be consumed.

Sweet Honey

The storm rocking outside our bedroom window grooved its way into my dreams and pulled me back into reality's weaving seams as I automatically reach next to me and it seems you aren't there.

Checking the time as I heard some noises coming from downstairs, I got up to see what you were up to; me and my messy 2 a.m. hair.

As I met the steps, I heard music becoming clearer with each stair, my feet cold and bare.

And following that sound I found that silly man over a filled cake pan and a goofy smile spanned both our faces while I took a seat at the counter chair.

He told me I gave him a bit of a scare.

With a little smirk on his face I gave him a playful glare.

Apparently, some serge of baking inspiration sprung right through him and he wanted to bake me honey cake to enjoy with coffee in the morning and we'd share.

Such a thought made me smile as he placed it in the oven and set a timer, always so prepared.

And then catching me off guard he scooped me into his arms and sat down in our large vintage armchair we got from somewhere.

I sat cuddled in his lap, the safest comfiest place in a 2 a.m. time gap, sweet honey filled the air as I now drifted off in the chair in the arms of the best care.

Do you ever feel so completely submerged
in a song and it's setting
that you could just die within it,
and you'd be perfectly fine with that
result?

Left in a mesmerized state
are the eardrums and soul,
and they'll have to take it up
with fate to consult.

Light Flooded Eyelids

Have you ever taken a nap under a blanket and when you woke up you can still see the sunlight underneath?

It ever so gently hits differently as it lightly soaks in beneath.

That's precisely you.

Simple and true.

I was hiding from the world, like one takes shelter from the cold, underneath decorative fabric.

I wasn't trying to be dramatic but of society and normality I was less than ecstatic, I was nearly almost in a panic.

But just as that light, you came shinning in, bright and careful.

Like a large blanket, I knew at times I could be a bit of a handful.

We've taken note of each other's flaws.

On good days and bad we have been one another's supportive applause.

You're my wild adventure book.

And I'll be the door handle you're happy you shook.

So, let's lay down together under the blanket and feel the fabric lightly heat from the sunlight poking through.

The inside of our eyelids lit, life is better than I could have imagined it, with you holding me and I holding you.

Good News & Good Weather

Let's do this.

Let's grab some food from the diner to go.

We'll take pictures of the things we'll miss.

We'll figure out a plan tomorrow.

For I am so uninterested in being a human lately.

For their molded expectations and lack of imagination makes no sense to me.

I am mesmerized by you greatly.

I would love to see you and me by the sea drinking tea that we both agree is more expensive than it should be.

You'll call home and tell everyone the sites we've seen.

You'll think it's quirky that I prefer to stay in contact through postcards.

But I kid you not most every place we stop has a postcard, even the small towns in-between.

But still you smile and kiss my head as I finish writing our regards.

Who knows when we'll go back, or who we'll grow to be.

Who would I be without the adventures we've had together?

You will always be good news to me.

You tell me I'll always be your perfectly prescribed weather.

I've seen a light, and I've dared to believe

that it belongs to me.

I won't let absentees in my strife

become the trustees of my life,

I will foresee my own reality:

I swear to the world around me,

and I don't care if it disagrees,

that it will be the most beautiful thing I'll

ever see.

Yankee Ingenuity

If we were present in the time where landlines ruled the nighttime you bet your dime, I'd have your number memorized.

Or when hangouts at the arcade were where memories were made, the best games were played, childhood debts were paid; we'd collaborate our tickets to get to the big digits to win the big prize but in the end we'd compromise.

If we were books in a library, I would hope we would be shelved in close proximity.

And if we happen to find ourselves as particles of paint hanging in a gallery I dearly wish to be in the perfect view of your imagery.

Maybe if we were pieces of thread we'd be intertwined in our colors in a beautiful quilt on the same comfy bed.

Or if anything instead, I hope I can be even just one sign of the good in humanity for you to see and believe; while in this life you tread, for you I'll always be looking ahead until you reach your designated homestead.

What I'm trying to say, in my own odd way, is whatever our essences happen to be I truly believe they're in fate's favor.

Whether we're at the aquarium and you're in one tank and I'm in the other, we're embedded in passing letters, or you're the brightest ray in the sun and I'm the darkest shade in the moon's shadow, we're always meant to find each other.

i'm feeling inventive today

i like me this way

you make me feel more than okay

the center piece of my heart's display

the clarity to my disarray

i'm feeling more in love with you everyday

This is my third voicemail tonight,

I know at this point you can't ignore the ones you've heard, but this ones right.

I was laying on the floor downstairs, before, when I called.

But I'm so sick of that ugly carpet; remember when we got this place, we swore we were gonna change it because man was that orange shag appalled.

We swore a lot of things,

Now the table is stained with neglected coffee rings.

Sometimes, for a moment, I'll see you within the circular shape.

But of course, it's my mind's mistake, it's just my longing thoughts trying to escape.

Ugh this is rough-

I'm tired of subconsciously trying to identify with everything, I just want to observe and live and that would be enough.

Your voicemail box will probably be full, and I should probably be sorry.

But, lovely, on the contrary;

I'm sorry I didn't replace the carpet, maybe I should just rip it out now.

I would have ripped out every outdated unwanted thing in this house, but I just didn't know how.

I should have replaced the wiring,

I should probably stop calling.

Typically, by now I have wine-soaked veins.

But tonight, I decided to match the coffee stains.

So, I'm on the empty wooden floor with a coffee mug beside me.

I'm not sure where you are but I'm sure by now you've put together that I still have my key.

But I don't want to bother you anymore,

I'll wipe down the table, leave the key, and lock the door.

I'm sorry that I failed, honestly, I just wanted to be your life's favorite detail.

Geez this is a long voicemail-

Cue the floodlights of my heart

The brain was not that smart

How was I to anticipate that at our start

You'd eventually depart

As your own hand pulled my foundation apart

While I beg for an irrelevant restart

You've already bid on a new piece of art

The Painter's Hands

I felt life in his hand when I held it.

Legit bits of perfect inspired grit, but he deems himself unfit, he claims I hold the permit of any life he feels but I simply won't omit.

For I've seen the shine decorated in his eyes when the day unveils a surprise or when he catches the sunrise.

He would not be given irises of a haven if he wasn't meant to glisten in an ambition that so easily becomes the ignition of a mission within the people around him to revise their deepened sighs and realize there's so much possibility and creativity underneath their dripping self-portrait skies.

Recently his default thoughts have brought out nothing but fabricated faults; his mind assaults him with false, harsh, critiques.

I don't care if it takes weeks, or tried and revamped techniques, I will help him seek the kindness and confidence his heart reserves and speaks for himself and I'll be here to assist in patching up any negativity leaks.

There's so much weight on those shoulders that he doesn't deserve, a weight that would entirely lose its physicality if he took away its ability to hold his anxiety against him; of course, I know from experience it isn't all easy to take over.

He just wasn't meant to exist quietly and I'm waiting patiently for him to see and the wondrous world to agree along with me that a symphony of imaginatively gifted life pulses and thrives within him, and he's the composer.

An ecosystem of wholesomeness lives in him, and he's very generous to give it out to others but I wish he'd receive some of his own.

Within that bloodstream lives a dream I know he'll redeem, and he won't be alone; I'll be here to celebrate every milestone and brace each leap of the intriguing unknown.

Because I felt life in his hand from the very first time, I held it and consistently since then.

I know we'll have adventurous stories to speak of, and his thoughts will be kind to him again.

I cannot chase people who do not want me

Even if I want them to

My energy isn't free

And I deserve company, that's love remains true

Holly Beach

Oh sweet Willy,

wont you take me to Holly Beach.

Let's be drily,

There're waves we need to reach.

I'll let you hold my hand if you carry me over the hot sand.

You can be the captain of this open water;

cooling off is the only thing we have planned.

Today couldn't, hopefully wouldn't, be much hotter.

Oh sweet Willy,

wont you take me to the city.

Let's be busy,

there're sites that need our observant pity.

I'll let you be witty if you call me pretty.

You can be my certainty;

dreaming will be our shared committee.

Today, with you, makes me so giddy.

Oh sweet Willy,

wont you take me to wherever you want to be.

Let's be optimistically involuntarily silly,

there's no one else for me.

I'll let you put a ring on my finger if you let me hold you forever.

You can be anything you desire;

traveling with you will be my greatest endeavor.

Today will be the start of our entire, but we can start small with some swimming attire.

Because I am more than determined

to be more than okay.

I have declared it to be so:

my soul did not struggle to grow

precious flowers from woe's deep snow

to not show

that others may not borrow my presence without my say,

they may not take my colors in exchange for their grey,

they will not be footnotes in my life's well-worded essay.

I am my own magnificently choreographed ballet.

Sunflowers

I hope you have your own sunflower field someday

So whenever you feel in dismay

When negative thoughts refuse to leave and chose to stay

Or temporarily your primary colors have taken to grey

Your soul may have a place to lay

A separate place to feel the sun's rays and the wind sway

A simple spot for when life is more complicated than yesterday

I hope you have your own sunflower field, and I hope you know it's okay to not always feel okay

For your ache will decay

And you will receive ease you won't have to repay

Alright look,

I don't need to hear romantic lies again for the thousandth time in my life when I can just grab a pen and write them myself in my next book.

Peppermint Fields

We've lost our sense of time; we've become quite inventive.

Overlooked city limits signs became a vital detail in our divine design of our new retrospective.

Determined to create memories far better than any stories our forced upon fellow residents will repeatably monologue in our future nursing home.

But if we had it our way, I'd say we'd prefer to perish in the flourish of our homestead roam.

We weren't looking to hide from the world, quite honestly the world doesn't appear to be ready for us.

It's not ready to adjust to our radicalness or the things we'd like to discuss.

So rather than conform, we decided to set off to find something of our own.

A place that makes sense, where community pulls together instead of providing destructive offense, moments and experiences beyond the bursting life in our phones.

Until we find our destination,

The nation is our running inspiration for memory locations.

We'll float down forgotten rivers and dub them with new, well worthy, names.

Enjoying tamed bonfires when we can, and when we've run out of songs to sing, we'll find moving pictures in the flames.

Breezy dancing in peppermint fields.

Forgetting about the hassle of extravagant meals.

We'll climb the trees that want us to.

Misty mornings and neon nights will be the venues of the moments we want to pursue and our individual growth we've been building to renew.

As long as our hands can hold each other, everything else will fall elegantly where it may and that's okay.

We'll find purpose in every day,

We'll rewrite clichés,

We'll take on the miles of pathways,

Highways and railways,

Until we find our getaway to stay.

Groovy

I danced with the sunshine on the hardwood floor until it decided to sleep.

In the absence of its company the windy night whispered to me, secrets I can hardly keep, but I won't utter a peep for our bond runs deep.

It provides a dimness I can appreciate, and my appetite loves its cheap food.

And in its air, there is no judgment on how I should be viewed and cradles me in comfy solitude.

I've noticed my thoughts, and they're well aware of me.

It's been a lifelong affair, always there to remind me life isn't fair, but as of late we've set aside despair and we've come to agree.

No longer will I live in actions manufactured to please fractured people when they are less than able to understand me; this cycled and recycled disappointment is arbitrary.

I am not a mistake; my existence is extraordinary.

I will dance when given the slightest chance.

I won't care, in advance, if others steal a glance.

My soul has deserved unapologetic unconditional love from the start; though it breaks my heart I've deprived it of that for so long I swear I can feel it glow as I start now.

I vow as long as we're jiving, surviving, living, and thriving I will pour my whole love into it and grow and relearn if I forget how.

Somedays I won't be at my best, but tomorrow will calmly reassure me it's waiting there.

My thoughts and I will have mutual forgiveness as my soul tidies up the mess, they will all rest together; peace we shall share.

I'll always have my designated dance partner in the morning, and when nighttime comes rolling, we'll kick it for a while.

I'm just here to remind myself that I don't always have to smile, my healing is worthwhile, and kindness is always in style.

I looked out your bedroom window,

and I realized that I've seen almost every season's scene within its frame.

With each season passed, your name calmly claimed a place in my heart

and became the start of my oasis,

a part of my newfound basis;

I gladly wasn't the same.

I looked out your bedroom window,

and my mind declared that it didn't have a single bad perspective.

No matter the time of day it was always the right time to look through it

and seek a meekly profound introspective.

I looked out your bedroom window,

and I saw a peace I could finally feel.

The moments through it are so still,

leaning on its sill,

reminiscing our collected memories

that could be mistaken right off a movie reel.

Ode to Headphones

Oh headphones,

the run we had was nothing short of grand,

the countless hours of podcasts and music we've been through I'll never forget.

We flew to quite a few different states together,

gone through life disasters and happy days thereafter;

no matter where we went, we came as a set.

Oh headphones,

though the right bud was going your tunes continued flowing

whether the music was jiving or depressing.

Always there to capture the emotions I'm feeling and decompress my stressing.

Oh headphones,

every genre you had covered,

every favorite song you remembered.

Even in our departure you will always be treasured.

Rest in Peace, Headphones- September 2020

Life is somber Darling

but you

You're daring

redefining taboo

Classically refreshing

a timeless visionary

Nestled in your soul I'll be dwelling

I'm somber Darling,

You'll be the highlight of my obituary

Rotation of Fixation

i watched the headlights follow their own destinations

from my backseat reservation

the driver and passenger have their own conversation

there's a dead bouquet of flowers on the back dash, still serving itself as a wistful decoration

i can feel the highway's vibration

looks like it's going through its own set of renovations

this is the nighttime's population

it has no obligation

the moon has its set hours for visitation

we either fill it with our imagination

simply sit in awe and observation

or try to find protection

from our own realization of self-induced, anxiety produced, suffocation

And when my mind isn't being the kindest

and it's making me feel like the smallest,

there's something that I need to register.

I am not secondary,

on the contrary

this life better be ready for me,

because my imagination and obligation are in my favor:

I remind myself,

I am the main character.

Next Season

You keep popping up at the very worst time, course with your whole essence your presence never really has a place.

And if I let you in, I know you'll win, and my, the sin; I just can't begin it took everything in me to change how things had been, the pain you've scarred on me can't be erased its easily traced but you'd never guess by the look on my face.

I protect others from your repercussions.

I keep hidden that I feel a forbidden pull to your clutches of sharp and stinging touches.

People describe me as caring, always uplifting, and celebrating.

You would say I'm more a mix of deteriorating and devastating.

I would say I am someone who puts others before myself, which often is cautioned to only do within good reason.

But I'll do it every time, for I'm afraid if I don't, I may not be here next season.

Tomato Basil Soup

I'll make you tomato basil soup, and I'll hold your head.

I'll tell you stories that will give you good dreams before you go to bed.

No Darling I'm not thinking of leaving, I'm not going, you've had my heart from the very start.

I'd never want to miss out on a single detail with you, and that means every best and challenging part.

You're the greatest love I will ever hold and know.

I see you're the good in the world I thought vanished long ago.

Between bowls of soup and cups of coffee I will be your comfort when you need me.

Every day with you, no matter what we're going through, is where I'm meant to be.

Tomorrow has our names in mind, and the future can see it clear.

We met at the brink of love's hemisphere, fate has always been circulating in our atmosphere, we have many years, and you will always be my Dear.

January

In your darling company I appreciate things differently, and when you're not with me I wear your sweater.

That never fails to help me feel better, however, it also helps me to remember; when you're occupied with another endeavor, there's beauty around me that can't be traditionally measured.

The small details that life embeds so softly for us to cherish and discover.

The magnificently colored world we like to escape to when the light hits right through the sheets and under the covers.

How an artist tells a story through each picture.

How a writer paints an image with words and makes them last forever.

Now I see the beauty in winter.

Now I have more than enough reason to pull it together.

I appreciate the world around me, but I couldn't exist, to be, without your company; I'll always want and need you more than ever.

You're exactly what I imagined, all the days before I met you, when I dreamed of the day when life would be more than okay, where I was happy and better.

Enough is Enough

How did creatures with hearts stray so far away,

To think they are above the breath of someone else,

to take it so disgustingly away.

Humanity is crying,

was crying,

done crying-

now you'll hear us screaming

because tears are too transparent.

You will hear our words,

you will see our actions

because we refuse to let this injustice be passed down for the future to inherit.

We are humans,

we are souls,

and we need to protect and defend those who are in danger.

Equality doesn't want to hear your apology,

because sadly it looks at this country and sees a stranger.

It is disgusted with this poor quality of democracy,

When did safety become a monopoly.

If you don't see it as your duty to stand up for those who are merely just trying to live,

that only have the difference of their skin,

then you need to see this as a sign.

A sign that humanity and equality may come free to you, as it should be for everyone,

but it has been stolen from others- as if at birth, freedom is assigned.

This is your sign to stand up, to defend, if you're uncomfortable you should be,

racism and inequality should not, and CAN NOT be our reality.

You cannot say you love this country, that you stand for this country, if diversity is something you refuse to see,

if you are silence's faithful devotee.

This oppression is long overdue to shatter.

As a child we learn everyone is equal,

apparently, this lesson needs a sequel;

but the course title is changing because to say the system is breaking is more than understating,

history will know where you stood, class has been in session way before this aggression-

this is Black Lives Matter.

To become more informed & start making a change please visit:
https://blacklivesmatter.com/

Sunday Song

Dancing with you feels like some other form of existence.

I shall hold onto it tightly, because I don't take your presence lightly, and the universe must have thought highly of us together, and I admire its persistence.

How is it possible that the world is able to look and feel entirely different, even after decades of living it through?

There's a joined compound of lovely in the air to be found, details that deserve attention laying in the background, there's so much to be crowned profound, it's all because of you.

You're my cause for celebration.

My heart's one and only standing ovation.

Within your company my reality feels on a permanent vacation.

I am thankful for our narration, and you will always hold my upmost adoration.

I will hold you earnestly through harmony and absurdity, your heart and soul will be held carefully.

For I love you dearly and sincerely with all my certainty.

Killing the one thing we can't afford to lose with our own assortment of amuse, a musically filled cruise, deep conversations paved and engraved in their own avenues.

When you live with your muse the day is always destined for good news, and even if once in a while it reports the blues it's still you, every day, I chose.

I feel pretty lucky to be in your atmosphere.

I'm prepared for all our years, hold on my Dear.

I found the one thing that's gonna last forever, this is right where we belong.

We're just two people, happily wandering life, in a Sunday song.

Where She Goes, I Go

What was the last song that was stuck in her head, I'll never know.

In my queue will always be her favorite show.

Her love was the greatest thing I'd ever been bestowed.

I don't know if she knows my heart wasn't something she borrowed.

For she took it with her; where she goes, I go.

I'll find a new solo tempo, holding her photo.

She can't physically be in my tomorrow.

She dissolved somewhere I cannot follow.

But she's with me in every other way, I'll find a way to make it through the day in a way that would make her proud while she holds my heart in the earth's nurturing shadow.

Her glow continues to radiate my heart while we're temporarily apart; she's growing flowers and someday I'll follow bellow.

New Heir in the Air

There's something magical about the whimsical imaginable ideas that sprout in our shared mind while sharing this bed and space.

And as each one takes its rightful place in our creative database; I can trace the timeless excitement on your face.

What can we not do together, what can we not weather?

Surprisingly for those around to see it came naturally for us to make each day better and better.

In them I've found a refuge, that's transformed the dark that had its hold on me for so long into the light I always knew was there.

And in me they felt a safety, that grew in their confidence to live freely; to each other we showed care, and our futures declared a new heir.

Because there's something amazing and mesmerizing in growing and flowing with your person.

The world is wide and open, and loneliness is no longer our burden.

Empath

I'm so empathetic to the point where it hurts, and I think that's why I keep rewatching movies and shows.

Because I know what's going to happen, I'm well prepared; my heart can't take anymore blows.

It's not an emotional intelligence competition to see who has more emotion; I wish us all well, and I wish we all inherited some peace.

I'm just waiting and praying for that mystery chamber of serotonin to release.

I want a good world for my niece, and I want my future children to look up and be proud of the hero that they see.

But when I say look up, I mean into a mirror, I'm not talking about me.

Because I wish someone had told me I don't need to wait to have security, I need to build it inside of me; the world doesn't have to be scary, I can be invited to life's party without feeling like I have something I owe.

I'm going to continue to grow, I will find an optimistic not just a photogenic rainbow, I will be more than a pretty photo; someday I'll start a new show.

I wish I could go back

and tell my younger self

that I turn out

to be the main character.

But I suppose she'll grow up

and find out later,

and maybe that's best for her.

"Amongst anxieties and strife, I hope you have a safe happy place in your life."

Sincerely,

B.A. McRae

Follow B.A. McRae's journey on

Facebook Instagram Twitter

@b.a.mcrae

www.ingramcontent.com/pod-product-compliance
Lightning Source LLC
Chambersburg PA
CBHW022019290426
44109CB00015B/1235